ISBN: 9798337935812
Imprint: Independently published

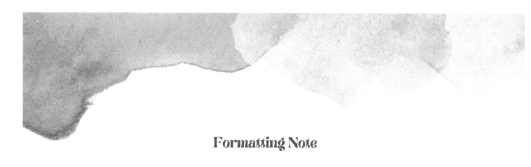

Formatting Note

Throughout this book you will find opportunities to make notes, or perhaps write some poetry yourself . Use it as a sounding board to spark your own creativity, whether you are writing a rebuttal to a poem or something new. I hope that you will choose to also have an experience as you read, that is as unique to you as these poems I share are to me. As a note to the reader, I have changed the page design so that a longer poem will be on the same style of page. This meant to substitute numbering each poem since I didn't title any of them.

Nature and the Human Experience

The feeling of your stubble on the back of my neck
Rough, but soothing
Eliciting a tingle down my spine
How I long to feel you trace my skin with your lips
Bringing me to a state of longing
Hot and wet with anticipation
For more
For all that I can take
So that I can melt into you

And when we come together
Limbs encircled in a timeless dance
Skin to skin
A feeling of oneness
That expands into a blissful peak

Pulling apart reluctantly
Only for a moment
Then coming back together
And oh, as I lay in your arms
Running my fingers through the hair on your chest
I know there will never be enough to satisfy the hunger
To quench the thirst of my desire for you
So please, touch me again
And again, and again

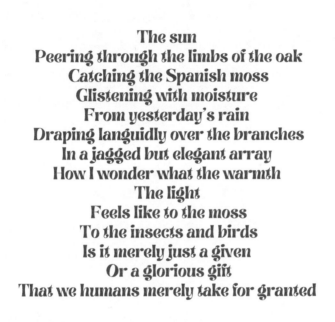

The sun
Peering through the limbs of the oak
Catching the Spanish moss
Glistening with moisture
From yesterday's rain
Draping languidly over the branches
In a jagged but elegant array
How I wonder what the warmth
The light
Feels like to the moss
To the insects and birds
Is it merely just a given
Or a glorious gift
That we humans merely take for granted

Go to the beach for peace
For the kind of grounding that feels elusive
Where all the clarity one seeks
Is present as the waves crash
Filling the spaces between sound and silence
If only you are open to listening
And when the wisdom fills you
The serenity so desperately sought will coalesce
From the threads in your mind
And the certainty in your heart
Into the knowledge that you seek

Time spent apart
Weighs on my mind
But sharpens my senses
Things that I perhaps wouldn't notice
Become apparent
Sharp and clear
Stronger than I knew to be possible

And so, when I hear the smile
Coating your voice across the many miles
A timbre all it's own
I can clearly see your face
The play of your lips
The gleam in your eyes
Full of love and delight

When I lay my head on my pillow
I close my eyes
And feel the warmth of your arms
Wrapped in a phantom embrace
That is so close to reality
So tantalizing and concrete
It is disconcerting to realize
That you are not here

How is it that I feel you now
As though your body is next to mine
Warm and inviting
Your scent lingering
Hours, days after
And no amount of distraction
Dissipates the allure
The craving to breathe you in again

Will I ever forget
The rhythm of our bodies
Moving together in harmony
As we make love
I don't know
But ask me again
The next time I hold you
And the answer will always be never
Never, will I ever, forget

notes

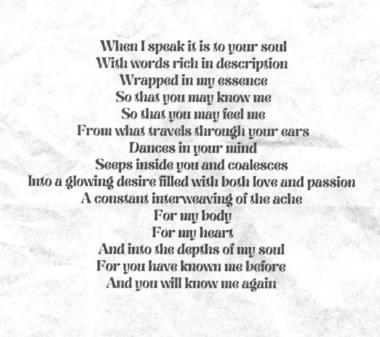

When I speak it is to your soul
With words rich in description
Wrapped in my essence
So that you may know me
So that you may feel me
From what travels through your ears
Dances in your mind
Seeps inside you and coalesces
Into a glowing desire filled with both love and passion
A constant interweaving of the ache
For my body
For my heart
And into the depths of my soul
For you have known me before
And you will know me again

Deep emotions are like grass
Patches die when covered
By the weight of something heavy
Or due to the lack of light

When you become aware of this
The dried up, brittle remains
Of what was once vibrant
Now manifest as a visible scar

Walking the expanse
Can you point to a spot
And say this is where he hurt me
This is from the time when she lied

Do you know your heart so well
That you can see and name
All the wounds real or imagined
And then, embrace them

Will you rid yourself of the weight of burden
Look to the sun
Water, seed, and fertilize the bare spots
Expecting all to be well in time

Or will you always have this reminder
Saying to hell with a perfect lawn
I can never let go, never forget
The ugliness here represent valuable lessons

Some days I can dig my toes into the dead grass
Feel the crunchy, dried up stalks
Then lament the loss of that beauty
Before rolling through the lush green that remains

Today, the clouds mirror my mood
They are dark, heavy, and foreboding
They threaten a great release of rain and thunder
Just as my heart threatens to open the floodgates
Unleashing tears, anger, and the desire to let go
The desire to give in

What do I hold so tightly in my chest
That feels as ominous as gray rain clouds
It should just simple to recognize
Nothing is so simple though
I'll toil away the hours trying to understand exactly why
To assign blame or responsibility

The boom of thunder deafening to the ears
Rattles me as much as my fears
Is it true that I am nothing but a blip
That I can make the biggest impact, but only for a moment
That I will easily be forgotten or replaced
Does it even matter enough to worry now

The flash of lightning seems close
I know in a minute, it will surround me
Burn the ground around me
Leaving a visible reminder of how fast it came and went
Stunning me to my very core
Just like the moment when first we kissed

And as this weather strengthens its presence
I say to myself
Who is really the storm here
You rolled in and swept me up
In a tumultuous cyclone of desire
Leaving me stranded out in the open

So now that I'm put in the elements
I want to cower behind the first bit of shelter
But I know in order to survive this
I must be present, I must be strong
Holding my head high now
I will tell you that I am the storm

How do you
In the same span of time
As short as a single breath
And as long as a lifetime
Allow me to feel that I am everything
And then nothing

I lost myself in your fire
Made room for all your quirks
Opened my heart to love again
Only to realize that I am a blip on your radar
A distraction from your worries
Another notch on your bedpost

I am the love letter you started to write
And on a whim wadded up and discarded
Using whatever excuse
Whatever out you could find
To recapture your energy
While siphoning off the rest of mine

I'm standing in the hole you asked me to dig
The one that isolates me from others
The one that keeps me in a prison
So that you can collect me later
When you desire another stroke for your ego
And expect me to climb back into your web

What you don't know
What you never bothered to find out
Is that your casual disposal of me
Has hardened me against you
You will never again feel my love
My love exists for greater things

notes

When you awaken
Reaching for someone to hold
What do you seek
Is it the warm, soft shape of a woman
Any woman that you'd bring to your bed
Is it her
Is it me
Is it the phantom of an ideal that can never be

If you could reach out
Find yourself
Wrap your arms around to comfort
Your aching heart
Your longing soul
Would you choose yourself
Would you take the leap
And love the one who can never leave

Do you ever look at yourself
Shaking your head in disbelief
At the hollow stranger you've become
The darkness of the years haunting your eyes
Casting shadows over your inner light
Stealing away the spark
The drive you once had
To be whole, to be great, to be wanted

When you lay in bed
Remember that entangled limbs
Whispered promises
Heated kisses
Are things you experience
But they do not define your worth
Missing these moments should not lead
To the loss of yourself

What is happening
I feel my world
Held together by so little
Now crumbling

I deeply desire
Freedom at all costs
I long to unload my mistakes
Even the long term commitments

Busting at the seams of this confined space
I need out
I need more
What if I could wake up

Remembering nothing of who I was
Remembering nothing of what I have to be
Would that fix it all
Could I finally be free

In my touch
Can you feel the tenderness
The soothing reassurance
The trickle of energy across your skin
Soak it up
As a sponge does water

Breathe it in
Immerse yourself
Wear the comfort I give like a coat
Wrapped tightly around you
On the coldest of nights
And know that I will warm you

As you lie here
Helpless in my arms
I want you to know
You are safe
I will hold you
As your battle the darkness

When the sun peeks through the curtains
Shrouding you from the light
Open your eyes to the warmth
Your heart to healing
Your mind to possibility
Your soul to the clarity you seek

Today I made a decision
I decided that it was okay
It's okay for me to let go
There is always yet another thing
To commit to doing
And I don't have to do that

The stress is not worth it
The benefits and satisfaction minuscule
I am so used to never saying no
So used to taking on more than I can chew
And today I let that one thing go
Now it is time for you

Let something go today
It doesn't matter how small it is
It only matters that it creates more space for you
That it relieves a burden
That you feel like you can breathe
Just a little bit deeper

notes

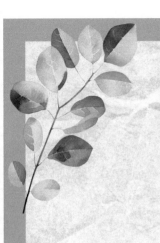

I have permission
To embrace my desires
Wrap my sexual energy
Around me like a silk robe
To be worn open
Or neatly tied closed
With the skin peaking out
Projecting my allure
Eliciting your desire

I am allowed to be sensual
To flaunt my curves
To use my touch
To speak to you
In a low come hither tone
And to stoke the fire I start
Until it burns hot enough
That we are both sweating in anticipation
Of what is to come

Every breathe
Every caress
Every moan and whimper
Pouring out of me without filter
Is my gift to you lover
And my gift to myself
As I fall deeper into the experience
And you sink into the bliss
That is with me, for me, inside me

I lay here now
Thinking of your touch
Firm, yet tender
Traveling the path of my body
Finding handholds and footholds
Along the length of me
As though you are climbing,
Traversing a mountain
Until you reach the summit
The peak of our connection
Where you place your flag
Lay claim to this place
This space that is my body

And as I submit to you
I feel you relaxing
All the barriers
All the secrets and insecurities
Lodged in your heart
Tucked away in your brain
Your secrets become known to me
Seeping into my skin
From the heat in your hands

The openness of your caresses
Tell me everything I need to know
All of your darkness
All of your dreams
Revealed to me
I see it
I feel it
Your capacity to love
Greater than you know
Greater than you allow yourself to believe

And all of this experience
Starting with a single kiss
Unfolding as you lay me down
Trace my contours and curves
With a lover's familiarity
And dance with me
Across the surfaces
Room to room in our delight
In our enjoyment of one another
Minutes or hours of contact
Leading to the desired conclusion

So I lay here now
Remembering those times
And I realize
In the quiet moments
When you are sleeping
That's when I swear I can hear it
The words of love and devotion
That remain unspoken
Bringing me assurance
That you will never just leave
Not without knowing you will be back

It's been a while
Enough time has passed
Each hour is marked with a sense of desperation
I am keenly aware of that undercurrent
And I sit here, considering
Wanting to call you
But I won't

I can't handle it
Can't handle the abrupt manner in which you dismiss me
Can't handle how small it makes me feel
Enduring your dark moods
Feeling like all you want to do is cut me off
Cut me down
I'm reeling from the high points
When you tell me how you love me
That I'm your everything
Then suddenly, you decide you're done talking
Done feeling and giving
You shut off and pull away

Sometimes I just wanna grab you
And shake you
And scream what the hell is your problem
Get right in your face
I feel like I'm tiptoeing around you
Afraid that if I misstep
I will set off a landmine
Honestly, it's so stressful that I avoid calling
What's the point in walking on eggshells
Where is the love that I feel down within my bones
When you touch me
Where is that need for each other
I know it's there
But we seem to lose sight of it constantly

I feel like I am being punished
For not being in the same physical space whenever you
want me
I am sad and drained
It makes me wonder what the hell am I doing to myself
Sometimes, I resign to the inevitable and start letting go
Then you reach out and touch me
My heart feels full
The blood starts coursing through me
Everywhere tingles
I climax in minutes, rattled to the core
The pleasure
The emotional release
Better than any drug
Laying in your arms
Riding the waves of euphoria
I know all is right with the world
And I soak it in
Knowing the cycle will never end
And I should be grateful for what I get

There's something about a rainy night
The sound of the wind and rain
Droplets hitting the pavement
Tapping against the windows
In a cadence unique to each moment in time

It makes me long to cuddle
To be wrapped up in strong arms
Bury my face into your chest
While nestling against your body
And listen to the melody of your beating heart

It reminds me of making love
The change in our breathing
The erratic beating of our hearts
The building of our ecstasy
Reaching a state of peak

Much like the weather tonight
Progressing from light to heavy
Until the intensity of the wind and rain crescendo
Then slow to a moment of pause
Stillness and peace descend

The rain subsides
Our breathing regulates
And time momentarily slows
The moistened earth feels nurtured
Our bodies remain intertwined in deep satisfaction

There's just something about a rainy night
That calls out to human kind
To dance in the ways we know best
To connect with the awe of nature
By experiencing what is natural

notes

His hands, deftly skirting
The edge of my satin slip
Resting at the top of my thighs
Draped delicately over my lap
Signaling a gateway to the soft, warm
Feminine pleasures that invite
Calling like a siren's song
In a sweet, melodic cadence
Not unlike the beating of our hearts

A moan escaping his lips
Hungry and primal with the desire
To claim, to devour, to possess
Making me ache for what is to come
Lips pressing against my neck
Hands in my hair, following the length down
Skirting my bare back
Tracing my curves
Settling on my hips

Please, I want to say
Make me yours
Touch me with the same energy
The same desperation as the first time
And the growing tenderness from the last
Like the next act in a great work
I am ready for the finale
And if I know you
There will be curtain call

Yes, that's right
Your body knows what to do
And mine knows when to squirm
Under the expert caresses
The trail of kisses down the back of my neck
All the cues that heighten the intensity
All the little sounds that fuel your desire
The evidence of my need for you
Moist against your body

As you brush against me
Cross the fabric line
Trace with your fingers
Circling around your desired prize
Before pushing your body against mine
Holding my hips
Sinking inside of me
In a shuddering, blissful moment
Where we both lose ourselves to the sensation

One snapshot of euphoria
After another and another
Just the sensation of being connected
Physically joined
Emotionally interwoven
In an act as old as time
But as new and joyous as the dawning day
Wishing these moments would never end
But also excited for the future

Weary to the bone
For countless reasons
Tackling one thing after another
Making sacrifices to get it done
Feeling disconnected from the experience
Lacking the needed flow to thrive

When do all the corners you cut
The paperwork you skimmed
The sleep you forfeited
Tangle together into the snarled mess
The mess, that you will label as failure
And wear like a scarlet letter

The tiny cracks in your poised facade
Showing occasional glimpses of your struggles
Threatening to overwhelm you with one misstep
Like a wave crashing down
Toppling your fragile castle
And washing away the proof of all your efforts

Where do you find any solace
How do you roll out of bed knowing
That you will always be exhausted
And you will never be or give as much as is required
To your work, relationships, dreams
Because you just can't

When you must be everywhere
And do everything
All at once
Your mind, body, and soul
Fragment into as many pieces
As you can muster

You must know that you're broken from your own devices
Somehow you thought you could manage
Believed that when this was all over you'd be okay
All the pieces of yourself easily coming back together
To make you strong, happy, whole
But they won't

When you must be everywhere
And do everything
All at once
Your mind, body, and soul
Fragment into as many pieces
As you can muster

You must know that you're broken from your own devices
Somehow you thought you could manage
Believed that when this was all over you'd be okay
All the pieces of yourself easily coming back together
To make you strong, happy, whole
But they won't

Your new form of resilience will help you survive
But you will be a shell
A shadow of yourself
Dim from burning the midnight oil
Dull from not allowing yourself to shine
And never, ever able to be enough

Your arms
So strong
So welcoming
A place I love to escape
Where I know I am home
You feel the pulse of my body
The stress that I hold
The need that I have
To be held
To be released from it all

The stress of life
Enveloping me layer after layer
And you, lovingly peel away
All that keeps me isolated
All that makes me sad
Through loving caresses
Tender kisses on my brow
The sound of your voice
Whispering sweet nothings
And the promise of never ending love

When you make me lose control
In a beautiful, pleasurable, vulnerable way
Then pull me into your arms
Absorbing the tears into your chest
Feeling my exquisite relief
From your unwavering devotion
I know it to be the signature
Of a lover I've known before
One life after another
And most thankfully, right now

I feel the walls closing in
Will I be crushed by the weight of obligation
Or will I suffocate from having no room to breathe
Maybe I will drown when I tire from treading water
From every visible angle my demise is imminent
Only, it is just my sanity that suffers

Do you feel it too
The crushing weight of obligations
The unrealistic expectations
That no matter how much there is to do
How many obstacles that make it impossible
Still somehow you must succeed

And when you rage
Release the growing frustration
Scream and wail from overwhelm
You will only widen the chasm
The great gap filled with disdain
Highlighting your inadequacy

You will never do enough
You will never be enough
Because your children aren't perfect
And your house is never clean
It feels better to pile things around you
And hide behind what will never make you happy

Can we agree that sometimes
Or perhaps even often
Your continued shortcomings
Are just unacceptable failures
And you don't deserve a glimmer of joy
Not even a moment of happiness

Or is that just me
It's just me with the problem
No need to drag anyone down
Just try not to waste your energy
Looking down on me
Because I will always fail in your eyes

notes

The subtle ripples on the surface of a pond
Not enough motion to disturb
The algae around the periphery
Reachable at water's edge
Where the bank relinquishes solid ground
And slips underneath the opaque depths

What does this detail
This seemingly innocuous image
Bring to the mind of the onlooker
Is there some obvious truth
Will I study it and have a great epiphany
Or will I just let it be, enjoying it for what it is

Perhaps it shows that a lack of motion causes stagnation
That without it all the gunk will multiply
Spreading from the outside inward
Enveloping the whole of pond
With a slimy green residue
And deterring the onlooker from enjoying its beauty

And with this realization should we then infer
That this clue from nature is a warning
A warning to move and flow in life
To fight the tendency to let the debris encroach
To keep our minds and bodies clean
In whatever ways possible

Or is it just a pond
With a circle of algae skirting the bank
Something to enjoy because of the water
Something to love because of the sounds produced
Something to accept as a gift from nature
I suppose it just depends on the hour and the day

What straw will break this camel's back
I asked the whispering breeze
The more I long for freedom
The more I pile onto me
Hoping somehow I'll accomplish something
Something that's truly, only just for me

And as my body sinks further down
Buckling from the weight of expectation
I twist and writhe and wonder why
I feel so incomplete
Is it because I can't seem to get a single thing to be
The way it's meant to be

It matters not what I strive to be
Or what you think I am worth
There will just be one more thing to do
One more person to please
And no matter how I pile it on
I will never get to be truly, deeply, wholly me

A simple nod or thank you
Would not go amiss
And yet I know, no matter what
For me, there will be no bliss
For I long to do, and long to be
Completely free, of all of this

Tonight the air crackles with energy
Flashes illuminate the sky
Thunder crashes and booms
The rain falls in heavy sheets
It's not the time to be anywhere within reach
Of nature's thrall
But the beauty is undeniable

Will you share it with me
Cuddled close in bed
Skin to skin
Listening to the sounds
Feeling the pulse
During each bright flash
Admiring the silhouette of each other's faces

Will you hold me tighter
During the peaks of the storm
Wrapping around me
As if by doing so you shield me
Protect me from the elements
Communicating safety with your body
And allowing me to surrender to the moment

Can we use it as an excuse
To make love more passionately
To set aside all other worries
To flow with the rhythm nature provides
Just because it is the perfect weather
Or the perfect time to remember
Time keeps moving forward

I don't want to miss a moment
Even if there may be another storm
On another night we are together
This one is now
And tomorrow is no guarantee
So let us seize the moment
Instead of planning to live for another day

Tell me how
To capture the essence
Of those beautiful moments
Reflected in your starry eyes

Tell my how
To bring the intense joy
Or deep longing
Within myself

So I can taste the feeling
Savor it within me
And know the quality
Of that which fuels your dreamy state

I want to be lost
Immersed in the layers
Of elaborate emotions
And profound revelations

To feel and see
In a way I can not fathom
Exist on a plane that seems surreal
But deeply appealing

Maybe then I can connect
With the dreamer I long to reach
And the peace that eludes me
That is embodied within you

notes

Eternal contentedness, bliss
That state of knowing that you're connected
With that which is greater than you
It's already within you
It's already all around you
Not in a building
Not in a box
Not in any structure or relic or memorial

It's within you and all around you
Your connection with the spirit of the Earth
Your connection with nature and all its beauty
Connect with them to find your heaven
Sink your feet into the dewy grass
Feel the resonating energy of the universe in your very cells

Never will you find it in your corner church
Never will you find it in a book written by any man or woman
Never will you find it through blindly following others' values
This never ending quest traveling the hamster wheel
It does not serve you
It only makes you feel deprived, inadequate

Why do we let this happen
Why can't we trust in the knowledge of our body
When did we sign off on our human right to connect with that which is divine
When you feel this unrequited longing for unconditional love
When you feel this deep desire to be truly connected
With everyone and everything

Look within and look around you
Listen to the words of the trees, the animals, the plants
They have no agenda
Your connectedness with life and the universe
That is what you're missing
That is what you weren't recognizing
Step up and embrace it
Then tell me that there is no divine love
That we are all on our own and our actions are in isolation
I don't think you'll be able to
You will not be able to deny the deep vibrating truth within your core
The awareness that you are one with the energies of the universe
And by recognizing that and tapping in, finally you will feel at home

Dear potential partner
There are things I need you to know
Things I will never tell you
Because it cracks me wide open
To admit this weakness
To air this vulnerability

I feel bolstered from your contact
Validated by our exchanges
That yes, even a mundane day matters
Because it's my day
And you want to share my experiences
Or at least you want to support my feelings

It's not that I want a captive audience
Rarely do I have much to say
But knowing you would listen
Knowing that you want to connect
That makes the worst day more bearable
The best day more brilliant

When I reach out to you and you ignore me
It makes me want to shut down
Then I stop reaching out
I wait for your cue to me
So I can eagerly respond
And not risk feeling rejected

It makes me wonder
Does it bother you that I wait
That I don't reach out first
That the days that go by are lonely
Do you think it's because I don't care
I want to believe it is just a safeguard

This distance keeps us safe
It keeps up from bonding
But maybe being safe is more important
I wish I could tell you this
And it would be so much relief
But I know that I never will

Curiosity primes you
To ask what you want to know
Looking upon the situation
With a detached, clinical air
That distance keeps you safe

If you are safe perhaps you can dig a little farther
Satisfy the desire to know
Experience something vicariously
Almost like a voyeur
Except you think you are pulling the strings

Watch me dance this dance
For the benefit of your knowledge
Wrapped in the safety of space
Space created to shield you
From any possibility of getting too close

Perhaps I am out to get you
Just like everyone else
Or certainly it feels that way
Let me assure you that you are wrong
I need all of my energy for my own survival

What is the purpose really of this
I feel like a lab rat being prodded
To see what I will do
Adding to your data
To what end I ask

Then I realized
It has nothing to do with me
And everything to do with you
You need to be safe
But you long to be connected

So carry on pushing your buttons
Drawing your distant conclusions
And see what you get from that
We all need to be safe
And the message is very clear

Casual and friendly
Don't expect any true revelation
My heart is genuine
And even a friend needs to respect that
Decide where you want to safely be

Purpose, a winding journey
Something we seek
Something that we adjust
Trying to accommodate
All the new ideas or new situations

This quest for purpose
It can feel very circular
Or it can feel like just the right push
Depends on who you ask
Sometimes even the day you ask them

When I reflect on purpose
It turns me inside out
It makes me question everything
My motivation, goals, and progress
It exposes me to all my shortcomings

I wonder why I do it to myself
Under the guise of always improving
Or wanting to live in authenticity
Maybe it's to kickstart myself
Along a path I have been afraid to walk

So if you see me brooding
Muttering about why, what, or how
It's likely due to some roadblock
Some sharp curve in the road
That ultimately influences my sense of purpose

By saying this aloud
Does it lead you into your own dark corners
Those secret places that don't get enough light
Or will you be able to charge forward
Confident that your sense of purpose never wavers

notes

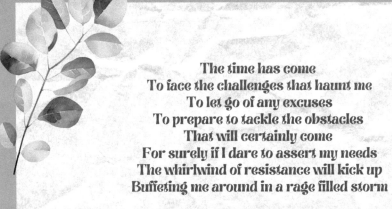

The time has come
To face the challenges that haunt me
To let go of any excuses
To prepare to tackle the obstacles
That will certainly come
For surely if I dare to assert my needs
The whirlwind of resistance will kick up
Buffeting me around in a rage filled storm

I deserve nothing if it doesn't suit you
My role is to struggle and survive
Being free and happy is not an option
How dare I have other goals to pursue
Not if it means more work for you
I should forego my happiness
Suffer a long and lonely life
Just stay and keep the peace

It's not okay to want love in my life
Being held is a luxury I don't deserve
Wanting emotional connection is insanity
I should just keep my head down
Meet my obligations with quiet dignity
Stop rocking the boat that will easily capsize
When the next big wave hits
Crashes inward with the ferocity of my repressed needs

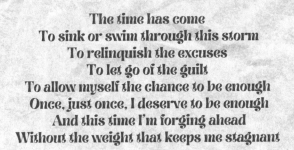

The time has come
To sink or swim through this storm
To relinquish the excuses
To let go of the guilt
To allow myself the chance to be enough
Once, just once, I deserve to be enough
And this time I'm forging ahead
Without the weight that keeps me stagnant

All this time
Years when perhaps I could
Perhaps I would
Have known a better life
I realize I can't get that back
All I can do is fight for what's left
I'm ready to row
No time like the present

Congratulations to you
The mastery of behavior
Capturing the essence of a petulant child
You have that down pat

When does being hateful
Or calling someone names
Become a go to behavior
For any reasonable adult

I must have missed that memo
And you're crazy if you believe
That I will just stand by
And not vehemently protest

Thanks for reminding me that your ego
And your insurmountable insecurities
Give you the go card
To behave however you wish

But how dare I not jump like a trained animal
Whenever you need to be coddled
That's surely deserving of hatred
Of the verbal spewing that leaves its mark

The desire to flatten your ego is brewing
I will level you with the reality
That I am not here to absorb your wrath
Or solve the problems you create for yourself

Let's just be casual about this
I want to go along with it
But, sex isn't casual
At least the kind that I desire
But I suppose, touching our bodies
Skin to skin, in places usually covered
Or the intermingled sweat
Is something you expect to feel with anyone

Feeling you inside me
And how our bodies fit together
Doesn't feel casual
When my body opens to yours
It reveals endless truths
If you paid attention you'd realize
Not only can you know my body
But you can know my heart

Surely the commitment it would require
To bring someone any depth of pleasure
Outweighs the satisfaction of knowing
That you did that for them
You released mountains of piled up stress
Facilitated a momentary connection to spirit
Opened them up to a state of knowing
A bliss rarely ever achieved otherwise

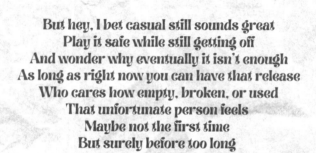

But hey, I bet casual still sounds great
Play it safe while still getting off
And wonder why eventually it isn't enough
As long as right now you can have that release
Who cares how empty, broken, or used
That unfortunate person feels
Maybe not the first time
But surely before too long

Choose your battles wisely
The effort to stay disconnected will haunt you
In the many lonely hours
Building up in your future
Because there is nothing casual about intimacy
No short cuts or barriers that will produce
The quality you claim you seek
All the while, keeping it casual

The anticipation of the first touch
Your fingers caressing my palm
Or brushing against my neck
As you gently sweep my hair back
To stroke my cheek
I blush just thinking about it

My secret ache to feel your skin against mine
Your lips pressed against my neck
Hands tangled in my hair
I can feel the tingle rise from my toes
Leaving goosebumps up the length of me
Every time I imagine how you will touch me

So much power you hold just by the promise
Of intimate moments to come
How did you creep into my mind
Hold me in your thrall with only words
My body seems to know what to feel already
And the pull of that is hard to ignore

Do me a favor, would you
Break me out of my head
And pull me into my body
All it takes is your touch
You will know what I need
I can feel your desire

Thinking about being in your bed
It's the sweetest form of torture
Because I know
I just know you will take me on a journey
From the ecstatic corners of my brain
Into the sacred depths of my body

notes

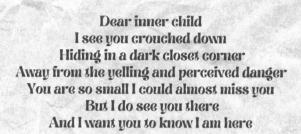

Dear inner child
I see you crouched down
Hiding in a dark closet corner
Away from the yelling and perceived danger
You are so small I could almost miss you
But I do see you there
And I want you to know I am here

I'm sorry for the lack of communication
For not getting around to you
As I continue to stuff down the feelings
That you were not allowed to have
Or punished for expressing
It's better to be tough
So much easier to stay disconnected

When I think about the ridicule
The relentless taunting you endured
Just because you dared to feel emotion
Because you felt sad and needed to cry
How weak and helpless you appeared
To the domineering personalities
Who only know how to be harsh

I want you to know I understand you
Shutting down was the perfect shield
Remaining stoic freed you from criticism
And as the years went by
It became easier to stuff down that emotion
To carry yourself with poise
Allowing the strain to remain under the surface

Can I talk you into unfolding yourself
Crawling out of the corner and into the light
You have the right to feel
Even if that means you're going to cry
I will keep you safe
I wish I had told you this earlier
But now I am ready to be what you need

So I will sit here waiting for you
On the floor outside your safe space
With open arms and open heart
You can cry until you are empty
I will hold you as long as you need
This is my commitment to you
And hopefully one day you will join me

Now that I realize
That I am deeply lonely
And terribly broken
I wonder if there is any point in this
Why keep striving for the next thing
When still I go to bed alone
And wake up to another round of chaos
A truly, and deeply unfulfilling world
In which I will never do enough

And regardless of what I try
I will not achieve the desired outcome
I can find no satisfaction
Or feel enough pride in myself
To fill this giant gaping hole within me
My roles are inconsequential
My heart feels strained from the weight
So much giving without any reception
Please tell me why I try

You can't explain away my feelings
With a shallow hypothesis
Though, it's convenient to say it
Perhaps my brain has a chemical imbalance
And I need to change my expectations
Or maybe have some gratitude
It could be worse after all
My desire for validation is inconsequential
My need for love a barrier to coping

I'm keenly aware that I am not okay
What do I do now
Walking away would be considered selfish
Having any dream that does not include sacrifices
Would be unheard of to those that judge me
I can feel myself cracking
I'm not sure how much more I can muster
Do I have anymore discipline
To fill in the cracks yet again

When I close my eyes
I feel myself floating along, somehow
I wonder when the weight will finally drag me down
When I will no longer care enough to struggle
Looking down on myself from above
All I can think is, oh that's so sad
I'm still trying to detach myself
From the reality that it is me
It is me that is so sad

Don't throw me a lifeline
I may somehow drag you under
Just let me struggle
But spare me more judgment
I have plenty of that without more scrutiny
I just wanted someone to know
Just wanted to give a veiled glimpse
Of how it feels to be me
So that I won't go down without one small ripple

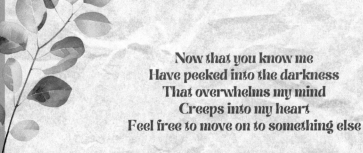

Now that you know me
Have peeked into the darkness
That overwhelms my mind
Creeps into my heart
Feel free to move on to something else

I'm not here to put on a show for anyone
I am not going to chase you
Or beg you to let me entertain you
I don't have the capacity to take on more
And I can't handle being easily discarded

The wounds that keep me detached
That allow me to intellectualize sex
Or search for a greater meaning without emotion
They are in that darkness that you skirt
And it keeps me safe from the next rejection

Trust me on this one
You don't actually want to know me
Not in the way required to have true intimacy
Supposedly you are seeking connection
But your risk of flight makes that impossible

I can feel your desire to run
It only takes the smallest nudges
And you shut down and retract
It's almost as though you live in a box
Afraid to ever venture outward

What exactly was the point in seeking my vulnerability
Did you want to try it on first
See if exploiting it would suit your needs
Gauge whether it would be a good idea to actually get close
Well clearly the answer to that is no

In the future be kind enough not to lurk
Not to watch the darkness like a voyeur
Opening someone up just enough
That unhealed wounds pour out of them
And then leave them to face it all alone

I am waiting for the next time
The next time I get to feel the magic
When my body opens like a flower
To the tender caresses of my lover
And in his arms I get to feel my power
The power to thrill another
The power to hold space for acts of love
The power to be the woman I intend to be

It feels like an eternity to do without
A bond deep enough to make me blossom
Trust that is rooted in many hours of safety
Pleasure that builds a bridge to the heart
I miss it like the plants need water and sun
I feel withered and paltry
Shrunken and yellowed
Undernourished from a lack of connection

How long can one wait in this state
Before dying down to the root
Rotting from within
Until there is no turning back
The death of a soul from lack of intimacy
Is the final destination for this ride
I feel like it is moments away some days
And on others, there is this residual well of hope

We all want to be connected
We all need to be nourished
We all deserve a loving caress
But still somehow there are obstacles
It could be attitudes or priorities
Situations that seem unsolvable
Or even something as simple as self-preservation
When the risk seems to outweigh the benefit

I have fallen from all of these barriers
Layed on the ground for days
Then somehow got back up
Living off the small glimmer of hope
That faint glow in my heart
Left by a lover's genuine embrace
So here I am waiting once more
Nurturing that need to be fulfilled again

notes

Can I admit it now
That my desire for approval is a chain
It keeps me stuck to situations that hurt
Allows me to remain vulnerable to exposure
Is the perfect hunting ground to siphon energy

You already know this though
All of the yous that have passed
In and out of my life
Benefitting from a taste of my desire
To be treasured by another

At least now I can make it stop
Pull that chain in close to me
File it down until I can break it
Seek value in a way that isn't dependent
On the whims of someone equally insecure

That's right, I said it
Your own sense of value
Your own need to be on top of everything
Is why you act so flippantly
It's why you pull me back in when it suits you

I don't need your approval enough
To dry up from getting so little
The droplets of emotional water
That you suspect me to survive on
Are nothing compared to how big this fire burns

My passion and drive to excel
It needs tending, but not from you
Not from someone so shallow
So superficial they can't really see
All that will be missed in life from playing it safe

I love the rain here
How it comes and goes on a whim
Never knowing how it will present
Will it be a languid drizzle
Or a torrential downpour

When I walk from the front to the back door
It can easily only be present on one side
Or maybe when I turn the corner
The sky goes from bright to dark
Morphing the atmosphere in seconds

I miss the rainy season
When it finally ends
The unpredictable weather creates interest
And something so natural
Can not be discounted

Creating moments of awe
And a great excuse to be still
The rain is a gift
I'm grateful that it's so prolific
Even when I forget the umbrella

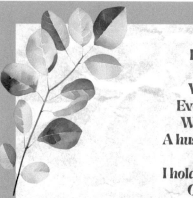

I don't want to be trapped
In this sterile container
Where obstacles prevent
Even the most basic intimacy
What I wouldn't do for a hug
A hug that is meant to comfort me

I hold children that are distressed
Or people who seek safety
But being held myself
The opportunity is so elusive
When did comfort become a prize to be earned
One that seems to take so much work

I understand why isolation is so difficult
When a morning in bed with another
Just sharing memories
Is something that can't happen
There is always a limitation
This makes the world very lonely to me

I remember when I thought I would have this
That feeling of excitement
When first experiencing some amount of closeness
Even the glimmer of connection
Then realizing that maintaining that connection
Requires cooperation and mutual effort

Just get me out of this container
Let me wile away the hours
In an intimate embrace
One that can sustain the stressors of life
And doesn't simply withdraw to survive
This current state of being can't be forever

The perception of color
How we all want others to see the same way
Name each shade to create a label
And that somehow creates cohesion

I like it best when I see a shade
One that I find so moving
Existing in nature instead of on a swatch
It makes me grateful that I have vision

All the nuances and details
That are captured by shape and color
It is hard to appreciate the natural beauty
When we can recreate it in a lab

But still it lacks the essence
The soul and the energy
That can only be found in living things
Regardless of our drive to be creators

Let us seek our ocean blue
Or grass green
On the palette our world provides
And enjoy seeing and feeling a color's beauty

notes

Acknowledgements

I want to thank everyone and every place that
inspired the poems on these pages. I especially want to thank those that have
endured reading them as I produce them and graciously serve as my sounding
board. There may be some things that resonate, some things that allow you to
escape into a moment, and some things that hit you hard. It is the same for me
when I write, and I am happy to share it with you, dear reader.

About the Author

J.P. Eldridge is a woman of many interests and works both clinically and in academia. She has been a lover of poetry for as long as she can remember. There is something about it's simplicity, intermingled with the ability to create depth that makes it special. This is her first foray into publishing her poetry on this scale and maybe one day she will revisit what she wrote as a teenager. For now, she will keep writing poetry and work on other genres as well. Stay tuned for other works in the future.

Made in the USA
Columbia, SC
28 October 2024

44934958R10041